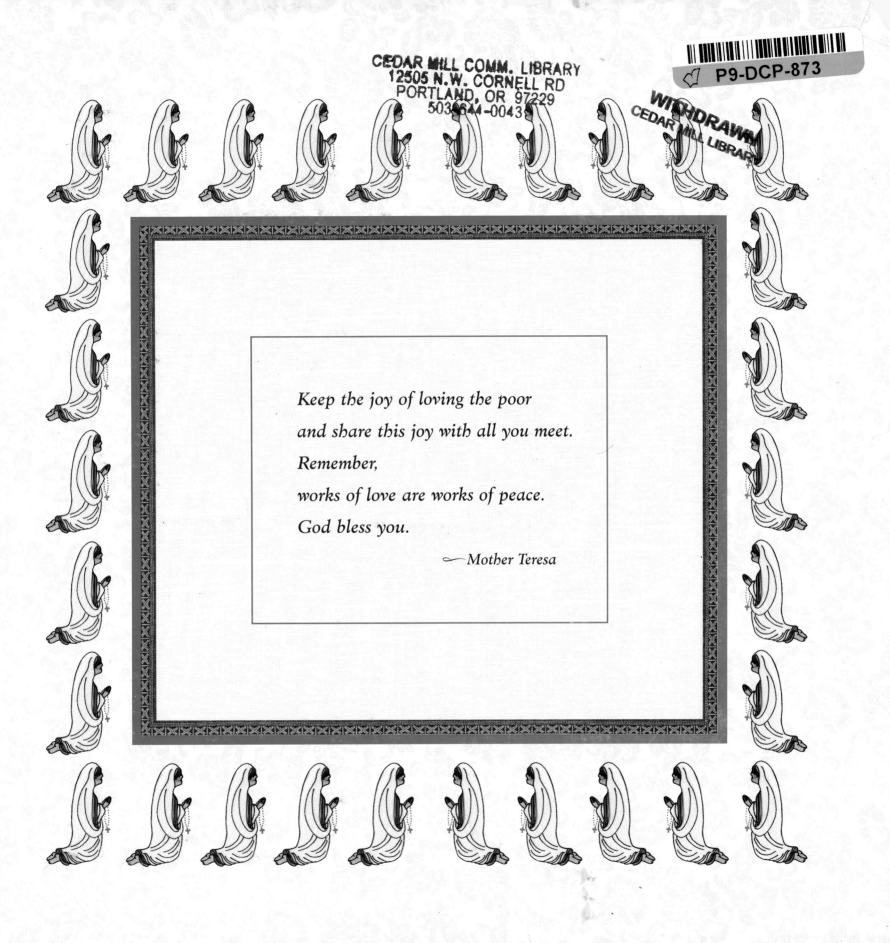

Keep the joy of loving the poor
and share this joy with all you meet.
Remember,
works of love are works of peace.
God bless you.

— Mother Teresa

Lord, make me a channel of your peace, that

where there is hatred, I may bring love;

where there is wrong, I may bring the spirit of forgiveness;

where there is discord, I may bring harmony;

where there is error, I may bring truth;

where there is doubt, I may bring faith;

where there is despair, I may bring hope;

where there are shadows, I may bring light;

where there is sadness, I may bring joy.

Lord, grant that I may seek rather to comfort than to be comforted;

to understand than to be understood;

to love than to be loved;

for it is by forgetting self that one finds;

it is by forgiving that one is forgiven;

it is by dying that one awakens to eternal life.

Amen.   ⌐Prayer of St. Francis of Assisi

MOTHER TERESA

DEMI

MARGARET K. McELDERRY BOOKS
NEW YORK LONDON TORONTO SYDNEY

MOTHER TERESA

was born Agnes Gonxha Bojaxhiu on August 26, 1910, in Skopje, Yugoslav Macedonia.

She was the third and last child of devout Catholic Albanian parents, Nikolle Bojaxhiu and Drana Bernai. Her father died when she was only nine years old, and later she wrote of her family, "We were all very united, especially after the death of my father. We lived for each other and made every effort to make one another happy. We were a very happy family."

At the age of ten Agnes attended a state secondary school in Croatia. There she learned about India through letters sent to the school by Jesuit Father Antony Vizak. He wrote vividly of the remarkable work of Catholic missionaries in West Bengal, and this inspired young Agnes to want to become a missionary and go to Bengal too.

One day when Agnes was twelve years old, she went to the chapel of the Madonna of Letnice on the slopes of Skopje's Black Mountain. There she felt herself called to a religious life—"to go out and give the Life of Christ to the people."

Agnes learned that the Sisters of Loreto, a community of nuns from Ireland, worked in Calcutta, India. She determined that one day she would go to Ireland to join them in their mission.

In 1928 Agnes left her family in Skopje and traveled to the Loreto Abbey in Rathfarnham, Ireland. Six weeks later she had received her postulant's cap, and she was so gifted that she quickly learned to speak English. Later on she easily learned to speak Indian languages, including Bengali and Hindi.

Agnes Gonxha Bojaxhiu chose to take the name Sister Mary Teresa of the Child Jesus, after the French Teresa of Lisieux, also known as "the Little Flower," who was declared a saint in 1923 and about whom it was said she did no great things—only small things with great love.

Teresa left Ireland and traveled by boat through the Suez Canal, across the Red Sea to Colombo, and through the Bay of Bengal to Calcutta. There she boarded a train north to the Himalayan hill station of Darjeeling, where, on May 23, 1929, she was made a Loreto novice and received her holy habit.

Teresa was sent to Loreto Entally, one of six Loreto schools in Calcutta. At St. Mary's High School for Bengali girls she taught geography and history in English. She also taught English as a second language to the Bengali students. Teresa loved teaching, and she called herself "the happiest nun in the world." Eventually she became the school's principal, and in May 1937 Teresa took her final vows in Loreto School, in Darjeeling.

As she worked in the convent school, Teresa became increasingly aware of her surroundings. Behind the high, protective walls of Loreto was Calcutta's worst slum—Moti Jheel, which means "Pearl Lake."

Moti Jheel was a shantytown, swarming with disease and misery. "How blind I have been!" declared Teresa. She began visiting the people who lived in the slum, trying to help them in whatever small way she could.

In September 1946 Teresa was on the train to Darjeeling for her summer retreat. "Suddenly," she wrote, "I heard the call of God—a call within a call. The message was quite clear. I was to leave the convent and help the poorest of the poor while living among them. It was an order, and I obeyed." September 10, 1946, thus became known as "Inspiration Day."

GOD SPEAKS THROUGH THE SILENCE OF THE
    HEART,
AND WE LISTEN.
THE PERSON WHO CHRIST HAS CHOSEN FOR
    HIMSELF—
SHE KNOWS. SHE KNOWS.
GOD SAYS,
I HAVE CALLED YOU BY YOUR NAME, YOU
    ARE MINE;
WATER WILL NOT DROWN YOU,
FIRE WILL NOT BURN YOU.
I WILL GIVE UP NATIONS FOR YOU.
YOU ARE PRECIOUS TO ME, I LOVE YOU.
EVEN IF A MOTHER COULD FORGET HER CHILD,
I WILL NOT FORGET YOU.
I HAVE CARVED YOU IN THE PALM OF MY HAND.
                                    ⁓ MOTHER TERESA

On April 12, 1948, the Loreto Mother General in Rathfarnham and Pope Pius XII granted Teresa permission to leave the convent. Five days later she went to the Holy Family Hospital in Patna, northwest of Calcutta, to study medicine. She worked with nuns, doctors, and technicians who specialized in obstetrics, surgery, emergency medicine, and infectious diseases. Teresa held patients' hands and comforted crying children. She went to the worst slums to aid the sick and the poorest of the poor.

Returning to Calcutta at the end of the year, Teresa put on the clothes of the poor—a simple white sari with a blue border—and walked into Moti Jheel. She gathered five street orphans and began her first "school" under a tree.

With a stick she wrote the Bengali alphabet in the dirt. She taught the orphans how to wash themselves with water and soap. Before too long this open-air classroom had thirty students. Caring people donated a blackboard, chalk, and some chairs to the school. Someone offered a house to Teresa, and many nuns offered their help. These small miracles proved to Teresa that God was truly with her in her mission to help the poorest of the poor.

Teresa became an Indian citizen in 1949, and in 1950 Pope Pius XII approved Teresa's new congregation, called the Missionaries of Charity, which vowed poverty, chastity, obedience, and wholehearted and free service to the poorest of the poor.

The nuns of the Missionaries of Charity lived on a plain and simple diet of bulgur, rice, vegetables, wheat gruel, and vitamin pills. Each had a metal bucket to use as a washbasin, one enamel plate, one spoon, fork, and knife, one bar of soap, one straw mattress, and one set of sheets. Each nun had three simple habits—one to wear, one to wash, and one for special occasions.

"All we do is for Jesus," Teresa said of the Missionaries of Charity. "We are first of all religious. We are not social workers, teachers, nurses, or doctors. We are religious Sisters. We serve Jesus in the poor, we nurse Him, feed Him, clothe Him, visit Him, and comfort Him in the poor, the abandoned, the sick, the orphans, the dying. All we do—our prayer, our work, our suffering—is for Jesus. Our life has no other reason or motivation."

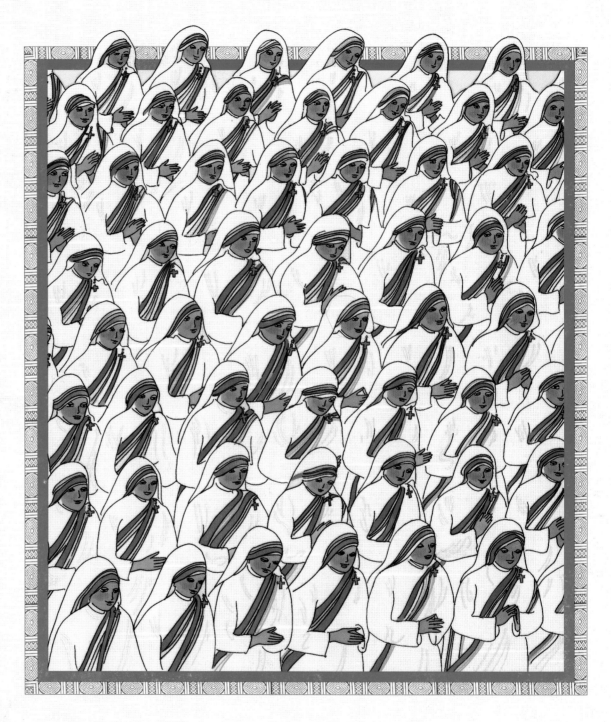

LIFE IS AN OPPORTUNITY—AVAIL IT.

LIFE IS BEAUTY—ADMIRE IT.

LIFE IS BLISS—TASTE IT.

LIFE IS A DREAM—REALIZE IT.

LIFE IS A CHALLENGE—MEET IT.

LIFE IS A DUTY—COMPLETE IT.

LIFE IS A GAME—PLAY IT.

LIFE IS COSTLY—CARE FOR IT.

LIFE IS RICH—KEEP IT.

LIFE IS LOVE—LOVE IT.

LIFE IS MYSTERY—KNOW IT.

LIFE IS A PROMISE—FULFILL IT.

LIFE IS SORROW—OVERCOME IT.

LIFE IS A SONG—SING IT.

LIFE IS A STRUGGLE—ACCEPT IT.

LIFE IS A TRAGEDY—BRACE IT.

LIFE IS AN ADVENTURE—DARE IT.

LIFE IS LIFE—SAVE IT!

LIFE IS LUCK—MAKE IT.

LIFE IS TOO PRECIOUS—DO NOT DESTROY IT.

— MOTHER TERESA

The training of the Missionaries of Charity was short, practical, and intense: The Sisters spent six months as aspirants, six months as postulants, and two years as novices until they took their First vows and became nuns. Intensive spirituality was taught through theology, church history, and Scriptures, but Teresa primarily taught others by her words and by her example.

"Never let anyone come to you without coming away better and happier," Teresa advised. "Everyone should see goodness in your face, in your eyes, in your smile."

Every day Teresa witnessed Calcutta garbage collectors carting away the bodies of people who had died overnight in the slums. She saw rats eating away at ill people who were too weak to move. She saw babies thrown away in trash cans. Her heart went out to these helpless people.

Teresa went to officials in the Indian government, saying, "What Calcutta needs is a place for the dying to spend their last hours. The dying should be able to die with love, consideration, and dignity."

The government offered her Kalighat, the rest house of an abandoned Hindu temple to the Goddess of Death, Kali. Teresa renamed the house Nirmal Hriday, which means "Place of the Pure Heart." This house for the dying opened on August 22, 1952, and Teresa said, "Death is the easiest and quickest way to go back to God. If only we could make people understand that we come from God and that we *have* to go back to Him! Going back to Him is going back home."

Teresa soon had so many Sisters in her missionary that she had to find a bigger home for them. Archbishop Perier of Calcutta found them a three-story building at 54A Lower Circular Road. In February 1953 Mother Teresa and her aspirants, postulants, novices, and Sisters moved into the building that became known as the "Mother House," and everyone began addressing Teresa as "Mother."

Mother Teresa patterned her own life, as well as the lives of her missionaries, on poverty. "We are poor by choice. We want to be poor like Christ, who, being rich, chose to be born and live and work among the poor. Let us do something beautiful for God by giving wholehearted service for the Glory of God and the good of our poor."

Mother Teresa was a great organizer, energizer, and galvanizer—a true leader with decisiveness, a clear aim, a plan of action, and speed in execution. Thousands of Sisters joined in her efforts, and she utilized them all as if there wasn't a moment to waste.

On September 23, 1955, Mother Teresa founded Shishu Bhavan—meaning "Sowing Joy"—a home for crippled, sick, and unwanted babies and children. Everywhere Mother Teresa saw thrown-away children in dustbins and drains. Abandoned infants, orphans, and handicapped children were left on railway platforms. All were suffering from acute malnutrition, tuberculosis, and a lack of love.

Many laypeople came to help Mother Teresa at Shishu Bhavan, bringing clothes and medicine and offering their time. Some premature babies slept in donated baskets, with the tiniest put in padded packing crates warmed by lightbulbs.

Shishu Bhavan also had a soup kitchen, a clinic, a dispensary, a shelter for unmarried expectant mothers, and an adoption center.

"The biggest disease today is the feeling of being unwanted, uncared for, and deserted by everybody," Mother Teresa said. "Outcasts are found at every stage of life, from the aged to the newborn infant. I have never refused a child, never. Not one."

AND WHOEVER RECEIVES ONE CHILD
SUCH AS THIS IN MY NAME,
RECEIVES ME.

⟳ MATTHEW 18.5

THE LORD SAID . . .
FOR I WAS HUNGRY, AND YOU GAVE ME FOOD,
I WAS THIRSTY AND YOU GAVE ME DRINK,
I WAS A STRANGER AND YOU TOOK ME IN;
NAKED, AND YOU CLOTHED ME;
I WAS SICK AND YOU VISITED ME;
I WAS IN PRISON AND YOU CAME TO ME . . .
VERILY I TELL YOU, IN AS MUCH AS
YOU DID IT TO THE LEAST OF MY BROTHERS,
YOU DID IT TO ME.

⟳ MATTHEW 25

Many people in India suffered from the disease of leprosy—a bacterial disease that attacks the skin. Hard lumps form around the forehead, nose, ears, and lips, and then the skin and softer bones are eaten away. Lepers lose their noses, fingers, and toes, and when their nerves are attacked by the bacteria, they die. Of the twenty million lepers in the world at the time, fifty thousand lived in Calcutta, but not a single hospital specialized in treating them. Mother Teresa knew that if the disease were treated in time, lepers could be completely cured.

Saddened by the fact that the lepers felt desperate and ashamed of their disease, Mother Teresa declared, "We must take the hospital to the lepers. We will go out in mobile dispensaries giving advice, medicines, and love." She started a campaign called "Touch a Leper with Kindness," bought five ambulances, and acquired much medicine. With her Sisters, Mother Teresa went to the leper slum in Titagarh.

First, the Sisters restored to the lepers their dignity and confidence by showing them how to bathe and bandage sores, to use the medicines, and even to perform minor surgery. The Sisters helped these lepers build their own homes and meeting hall, and they taught them practical skills like sewing, making shoes from old tires, basket weaving, brick making, and carpentry. Many of the lepers were completely cured after a year or two.

In 1965 the Indian government gave Mother Teresa thirty-four acres of land in the village of Asansol to start a leper colony, which she named Shanti Nagar—"Place of Peace." The Shanti Nagar colony was completely built and planted by the lepers, with houses, ponds, and trees. It was entirely self-sufficient, and Mother Teresa was proud to say, "This success was because of the amount of love put into it. And God sustained the love."

Support for Mother Teresa's work came in the way of financial donations that poured in from around the world. Presidents, kings and queens, dignitaries, and laypeople all donated money, as well as large foundations, which enabled Mother Teresa to establish Missionaries of Charity branches around India. The missionaries opened tuberculosis clinics, general dispensaries, mobile leprosy clinics, night shelters for homeless men, homes for the dying and the destitute, antenatal clinics, homes for abandoned children, nursery classes and crèches, and primary and secondary schools, and they established provisions for further education, such as training in carpentry, metalwork, embroidery, needlework, child care, and home management. They also opened centers for emergency aid in the wake of disasters, riots, epidemics, famines, and floods.

In 1977 a ferocious cyclone left two million people homeless in Andhra Pradesh, a coastal state in eastern India. When a tidal wave, floods, and devastation killed thousands more, Mother Teresa and her Sisters worked tirelessly to feed, house, clothe, and inoculate the survivors.

On March 26, 1967, the Roman Catholic Church approved Mother Teresa's proposal to establish the Missionary Brothers of Charity.

The Brothers' home was in Kidderpur, Calcutta, and they supplemented all aspects of the Sisters' work. They helped the Sisters with the lepers and took care of the men and boys in the home for the dying.

In Dum Dum, near the Calcutta airport, the Brothers set up a home for destitute boys, some of whom were later placed in boarding schools or studied as day scholars in local schools. Handicapped boys stayed at the home. Another home in Dum Dum provided shelter for the sick, disabled, and destitute.

Article 2 of the Brothers' Constitution directed: "Live this life of love by dedicating oneself to the poorest of the poor in the slums, on the streets and wherever they are found. Leprosy patients, destitute beggars, the abandoned, homeless boys, young men in the slums, the unemployed, and those uprooted by war and disaster will always be the special object of the Brothers' concern."

The Brothers set up a center for village work in Noyan, Calcutta, and cared for hundreds of poverty-stricken families, ran a primary school where children received classes and a daily meal, and treated tuberculosis sufferers. Another center cared for orphans and waifs abandoned on the platforms of India's railway stations.

In the early 1970s a group of Brothers traveled to war-torn Saigon in Vietnam and Phnom Penh in Cambodia to care for orphans, war widows, the crippled, the disabled, and the retarded.

Mother Teresa founded four more branches of the Missionaries of Charity: the Contemplative Brothers, whose lives were devoted to prayer and discipline; the Mission of Charity Fathers, whose lives were dedicated to serving the poorest of the poor; the International Association of Co-Workers, layworkers who served the poor; and the Contemplative Sisters, religious who prayed for the poor and the work of the Sisters and Brothers.

Ever since that fateful Inspiration Day in 1946, Mother Teresa placed herself blindly in God's hands, never knowing where she would be led or what she would be asked to do. She said, "I listen to the Lord and I have the gift of obedience. Because of that, miracles follow. From the first call, and the call within the call, my life seems to have a Divine Plan. Divine Providence is much greater than our little minds and will never let us down."

Numerous times, when it seemed there was not enough money to do the work of the Missionaries of Charity, money was donated to Mother Teresa from around the world. And when it seemed that the Sisters and Brothers might not have enough food to feed the poor, food was donated from around the world. It was these miracles that proved to Mother Teresa the existence of God and the importance of her life's work.

"I am nothing," Mother Teresa used to tell her followers. "He is all. I do nothing on my own. He does it. I am God's pencil. A tiny bit of pencil with which He writes what He likes."

BECAUSE YOU HAVE DONE THIS I WILL SHOWER BLESSINGS ON YOU.
I WILL MAKE YOUR DESCENDANTS AS MANY AS THE STARS IN HEAVEN AND THE GRAINS OF SAND ON THE SHORE.
— GENESIS 22.17

MANIFESTLY THE FINGER OF GOD IS EVERYWHERE. GOD PROVIDES. THERE IS NOTHING I CANNOT MASTER WITH PRAYER AND WITH THE HELP OF THE ONE WHO GIVES ME STRENGTH.
— PHILIPPIANS 4.12–13

Mother Teresa loved and was inspired by the Anima Christie Prayer of St. Ignatius of Loyola, a Spanish Jesuit who lived from 1491 to 1556:

SOUL OF CHRIST, SANCTIFY ME,
BODY OF CHRIST, SAVE ME,
BLOOD OF CHRIST, INEBRIATE ME,
WATER FROM THE SIDE OF CHRIST, WASH ME,
PASSION OF CHRIST, STRENGTHEN ME.
O GOOD JESUS, HEAR ME,
WITHIN THY WOUNDS HIDE ME,
SUFFER ME NOT TO BE SEPARATED FROM THEE,
FROM THE MALICIOUS ENEMY DEFEND ME,
IN THE HOUR OF MY DEATH CALL ME,
AND BID ME COME UNTO THEE,
THAT WITH THY SAINTS I MAY PRAISE THEE,
FOR EVER AND EVER. AMEN.

On July 26, 1965, the first Missionary of Charity Foundation opened outside of India in Cocorote, Venezuela. This was just the beginning of Mother Teresa's missionaries opening all over the world—and always in the worst slums, to help the poorest of the poor.

By 1987 Mother Teresa was overseeing 3,000 nuns in 358 houses in 80 nations. These Sisters, combined with the members of the various Brothers' institutions and of the International Association of Co-Workers, brought the number of her followers to 400,000.

One of Mother Teresa's vows had been to return God's love and compassion by loving Him in all of His distressing disguises. Leprosy was one disguise. AIDS (acquired immunodeficiency syndrome) was another. On December 25, 1985, Mother Teresa opened a home for men dying from AIDS in New York City, and she spoke out against the prejudice and ignorance that surrounded the disease. Hundreds more AIDS centers followed in many more countries around the world.

WHO IS JESUS TO ME?

JESUS IS THE WORD MADE FLESH.

JESUS IS THE BREAD OF LIFE.

JESUS IS THE VICTIM OFFERED FOR OUR
    SINS ON THE CROSS.

JESUS IS THE SACRIFICE OFFERED AT HOLY
    MASS FOR THE SINS OF THE WORLD
    AND FOR MINE.

JESUS IS THE WORD—TO BE SPOKEN.

JESUS IS THE TRUTH—TO BE TOLD.

JESUS IS THE WAY—TO BE WALKED.

JESUS IS THE LIGHT—TO BE LIT.

JESUS IS THE LIFE—TO BE LIVED.

JESUS IS THE LOVE—TO BE LOVED.

JESUS IS THE JOY—TO BE SHARED.

JESUS IS THE SACRIFICE—TO BE OFFERED.

JESUS IS THE PEACE—TO BE GIVEN.

JESUS IS THE BREAD OF LIFE—TO BE EATEN.

JESUS IS THE HUNGRY—TO BE FED.

JESUS IS THE THIRSTY—TO BE SATIATED.

JESUS IS THE NAKED—TO BE CLOTHED.

JESUS IS THE HOMELESS—TO BE TAKEN IN.

JESUS IS THE SICK—TO BE HEALED.

JESUS IS THE LONELY—TO BE LOVE

JESUS IS THE UNWANTED—TO BE WANTED.

JESUS IS THE LEPER—TO WASH HIS WOUNDS.

JESUS IS THE BEGGAR—TO GIVE HIM A SMILE.

JESUS IS THE DRUNKARD—TO LISTEN TO HIM.

JESUS IS THE MENTALLY ILL—TO PROTECT HIM.

JESUS IS THE LITTLE ONE—TO EMBRACE HIM.

JESUS IS THE BLIND—TO LEAD HIM.

JESUS IS THE DUMB—TO SPEAK FOR HIM.

JESUS IS THE CRIPPLED—TO WALK WITH HIM.

JESUS IS THE DRUG ADDICT—TO BEFRIEND HIM.

JESUS IS THE PROSTITUTE—TO REMOVE FROM
    DANGER AND BEFRIEND.

JESUS IS THE PRISONER—TO BE VISITED.

JESUS IS THE OLD—TO BE SERVED.

— MOTHER TERESA

In 1991, when Mother Teresa was eighty-one years old, she started to show signs of aging. She also had bouts of malaria. There was an extreme frailty about her, and with it came an even greater sense of urgency to continue her work with the poor. She contracted pneumonia, recovered, and continued to travel to the United States and Hong Kong to help the poor and open homes for handicapped children.

In November 1996 Mother Teresa suffered heart failure from coronary angina and underwent surgery at the Woodlands Nursing Home in Calcutta. Catholic Sisters and Brothers all over the world prayed for her, as did many Buddhists, Sikhs, Hindus, and Muslims. Again she recovered, then traveled to Rome to help and rehabilitate prostitutes, to the United States to receive the Congressional Gold Medal for outstanding and enduring contributions to humanitarian and charitable activities, and back to Calcutta.

On September 5, 1997, surrounded by her beloved Sisters in the Mother House, Mother Teresa died, called back home to be with her God.

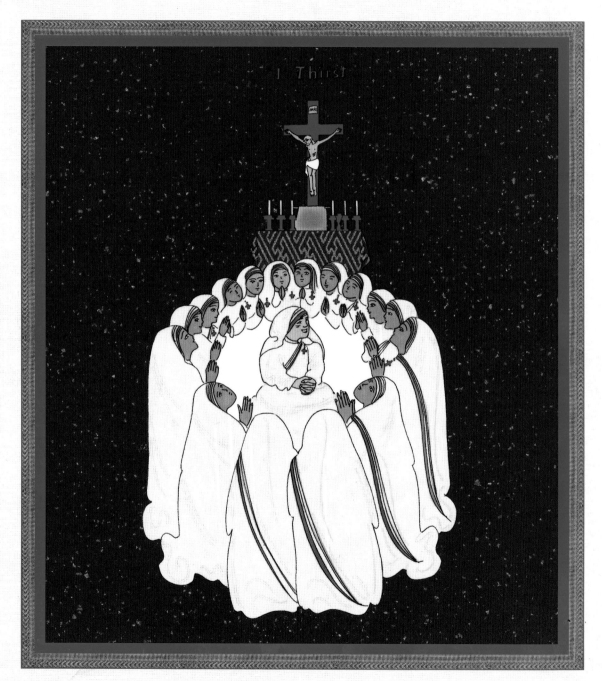

One week later India gave Mother Teresa a state funeral. Her body was borne through the streets of Calcutta on the same carriage that had held Mahatma Gandhi, the great peace leader, and Jawaharlal Nehru, the former prime minister. Tens of thousands of people lined the route to catch a glimpse of the woman who wrote on the fiftieth anniversary of India's independence from England in 1997, "When I look around India, the land God has given each one of us to call our home, I see so much of His blessings and goodness: in the smallest flower, the tallest trees, the rivers, the plains and mountains. But where do we find the most beauty of our country? We find it in each man, woman, and child."

Dignitaries from all over the world attended Mother Teresa's funeral, coming together from all religious and ethnic backgrounds to honor this great woman who had never turned her back on another person.

Mother Teresa left behind a legacy of forty-five hundred Sisters, four hundred Brothers, and countless spiritual workers, missionaries, and volunteers in whose hearts and work her spirit lives on.

It is possible that no one person has ever received more awards and honors than Mother Teresa. Always one to practice deep humility, Mother Teresa was reluctant to be singled out and given such honors. A living example of the motto "The more you give away, the more you receive," whenever Mother Teresa received anything—be it an award or food or money—she received it in the name of Christ's poor.

❖ AWARDS AND HONORS ❖

1962: Mother Teresa was honored with the Padma Sri ("Order of the Lotus"), a high award given by the government of India. In the same year she was awarded the Magsaysay Prize by the Conference of Asiatic States and was described as the most worthy woman in Asia.

1970: Good Samaritan Prize and the Kennedy Foundation Prize in the United States.

1971: Pope John XXIII Peace Prize at the Vatican.

1972: Pandit Nehru Award for International Understanding.

1973: Templeton Prize in London for Progress in Religion, from the hand of Prince Philip; and the Saint Louise de Marillac Award in Los Angeles, California, for charitable work.

1975: Albert Schweitzer Award for humanitarian work in the United States.

1977: Honorary doctorate from Cambridge University in England.

1979: Balzan Prize from the president of the Italian republic. She also traveled to Oslo, Norway, to receive the most famous international award, the Nobel Peace Prize.

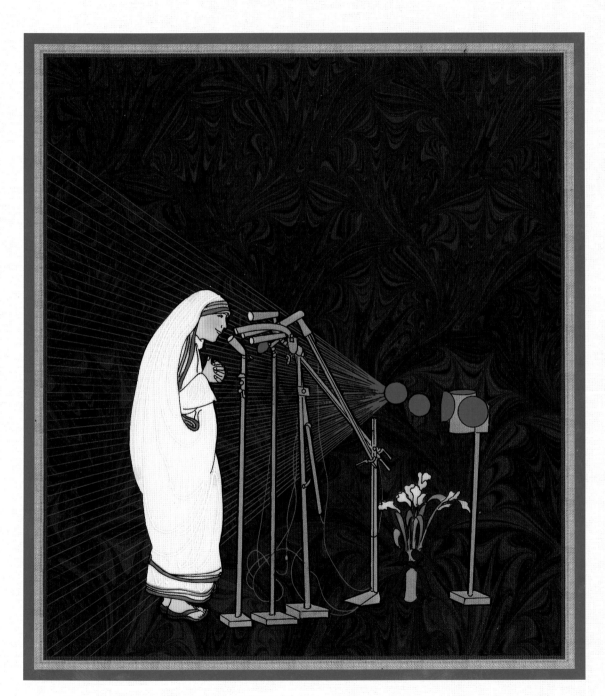

1985: Presidential Medal of Honor from President Ronald Reagan of the United States.

1987: Soviet Peace Committee Gold Medal for promoting peace and friendship among people.

1990: International Leo Tolstoy Medal, given by the Soviet government.

1992: Peace Education Prize from UNESCO (United Nations Educational, Scientific, and Cultural Organization). In the same year she also received the Gaudium et Spes ("Joy and Hope") Award from the Knights of Columbus for outstanding contributions to the Catholic Church and society and for her spiritual and humanitarian work.

1996: President Bill Clinton of the United States signed legislation making Mother Teresa an honorary citizen of the United States. President Clinton praised Mother Teresa for bringing hope and love to orphaned and abandoned children all over the world.

In her Nobel Prize acceptance speech Mother Teresa said: "Let us thank God . . . for this gift of Peace that reminds us that we have been created to live that Peace, and that Jesus became a man to bring that good news to the poor. . . . The news was peace to all of good will and this is something we all want—the peace of heart. It hurt Jesus to love us. It hurt Him. And to make sure we remember His great love, He made himself the Bread of Life to satisfy our hunger for His love—our hunger for God— because we have been created for that love. He made himself the hungry one, the naked one, the homeless one, the sick one, the one in prison, the lonely one, the unwanted one, and He says, 'You did it to me.'"

In 2002 the pope recognized Mother Teresa's healing of an Indian woman as the miracle needed to beatify her—to declare her to have attained the blessedness of heaven and to add her to the "Roll of the Blesseds." On October 19, 2003, Pope John Paul II beatified Mother Teresa of Calcutta. The recognition of another miracle is required for Mother Teresa's sainthood.

The following events are occurring in order for Mother Teresa to become a saint:

❖ Friends of Mother Teresa in Calcutta are promoting the idea of her sainthood to the local bishop.

❖ The Mother Teresa Guild has been formed to report on her Divine Favors, which are seven Gifts from God: Piety, Wisdom, Understanding, Counsel, Fortitude, Knowledge, and Fear of the Lord, resulting in a heroic level of love and all other virtues.

❖ A "Mother Teresa Newsletter" is circulating in Calcutta to alert the local bishop of Mother Teresa's virtues.

❖ The bishop of Calcutta is being asked to agree to Mother Teresa's sanctity and open an official inquiry into her life and deeds, performance of miracles, and proof of divine intervention.

❖ The College of Realtors in Rome are writing a historical biography of Mother Teresa that is based on information gathered from witnesses, the faithful, the local bishop, regional bishops, and the pope.

❖ Theological experts in Rome are to judge, verify, and certify Mother Teresa's miracles: Two times through Divine Intervention, Mother Teresa heard the call of God to go out and give the life of Christ to the people and to help the poorest of the poor while living among them. Other miracles included healings, rescues, and gift miracles of extraordinary provisions.

❖ The Vatican Congregation for the Causes of Saints is to verify and certify Mother Teresa worthy of sainthood and state that she was chosen by God to perform His work on earth.

❖ The pope is to issue a formal decree of Mother Teresa's miracles and proclaim that she can be worshipped as one of the church's blessed saints. The pope's decree of canonization will ensure that Mother Teresa is a Blessed Saint of God and will be forever after venerated as such throughout all of the Catholic churches in the world.

DUBLIN

SKOPJE

CALCUTTA

• MISSIONARY OF CHARITY FOUNDATIONS
⁓ MOTHER TERESA'S JOURNEY FROM SKOPJE TO CALCUTTA

To His Holiness John Paul II
and to The Most Reverend Alex J. Brunett, Archbishop of Seattle,
with great gratitude

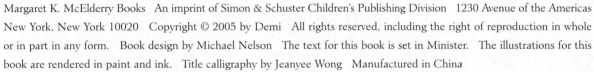

TEXT REFERENCES

Chawla, Navin. *Mother Teresa: The Authorized Biography.* Boston: Element, 1992.

Egan, Eileen. *Such a Vision of the Street: Mother Teresa, the Spirit and the Work.* Garden City, NY: Image Books, 1986.

Le Joly, Edward. *Mother Teresa of Calcutta: A Biography.* San Francisco: Harper & Row, 1977.

Le Joly, Edward. *We Do It for Jesus: Mother Teresa and Her Missionaries of Charity.* London: Darton, Longman, and Todd, 1977.

Spink, Kathryn. *Mother Teresa: A Complete Authorized Biography.* San Francisco: HarperSanFrancisco, 1997.

Margaret K. McElderry Books   An imprint of Simon & Schuster Children's Publishing Division   1230 Avenue of the Americas   New York, New York 10020   Copyright © 2005 by Demi   All rights reserved, including the right of reproduction in whole or in part in any form.   Book design by Michael Nelson   The text for this book is set in Minister.   The illustrations for this book are rendered in paint and ink.   Title calligraphy by Jeanyee Wong   Manufactured in China

2   4   6   8   10   9   7   5   3   1

LIBRARY OF CONGRESS CATALOGING-IN-PUBLICATION DATA: Demi.   Mother Teresa / Demi.   p. cm.   Summary: A biography of Agnes Gonxha Bojaxhiu, known as Mother Teresa, who spent most of her life serving "the poorest of the poor" in Calcutta, India. Includes bibliographical references.   ISBN 0-689-86407-8   1. Teresa, Mother, 1910– 2. Missionaries of Charity—Biography— Juvenile literature. 3. Nuns—India—Biography—Juvenile literature. [1. Teresa, Mother, 1910– 2. Missionaries of Charity. 3. Missionaries. 4. Nobel prizes—Biography. 5. Women—Biography.] I. Title.   BX4406.5.Z8D46 2005   271'.97—dc21   2003010128

FIRST EDITION

Lead me from death to life,

from falsehood to truth;

lead me from despair to hope,

from fear to trust;

lead me from hate to love,

from war to peace;

let peace fill our hearts,

our world, our universe.

Peace. Peace. Peace.

— Mother Teresa